D0613146

A Garden of Cats

Del Greger

Willow Creek
P R E S S

Published by Willow Creek Press
P.O. Box 147, Minocqua, Wisconsin 54548
www.willowcreekpress.com

Editor: Andrea Donner
Design: Katrin Wooley

ISBN 1-57223-596-9
Printed in Canada

When we moved into our house, we began landscaping the garden to the great interest of neighborhood cats. The cats would check in periodically, wondering what was happening to their former litter box. I began photographing them, and word soon spread to other cat owners with lovely gardens. I never met a cat or garden I didn't like, so this project has been enjoyable for me. Before I knew it, I had built a large collection of photos. In addition, I jotted down names and notes on each cat, which I share with you here. This book introduces you to my favorite felines — their personalities and habitats. I hope you recognize a bit of your own furry friends in the pages that follow. Enjoy!

When God made the world, He chose to put animals in it, and decided to give each whatever it wanted. All animals formed a long line before His throne, and the cat quietly went to the end of the line. To the elephant and bear, He gave strength; to the rabbit and the deer, swiftness; to the owl, the ability to see at night, to the birds and the butterflies, great beauty; to the fox, cunning; to the monkey, intelligence; to the dog, loyalty; to the lion, courage; to the otter, playfulness. And all these things the animals begged of God. At last he came to the end of the line, and there sat the little cat, waiting patiently. "What will YOU have?" God asked the cat.

The cat shrugged modestly, "Oh, whatever scraps you have left over. I don't mind."

"But I'm God. I have everything left over."

"Then I'll have a little of everything, please."

And God gave a great shout of laughter at the cleverness of this small animal, and gave the cat everything she asked for, adding grace and elegance and, only for her, a gentle purr that would always attract humans and assure her a warm and comfortable home.

But he took away her false modesty.

Miranda is the perfect cat model. She gracefully sashays into poses, holds them until she hears the click of the camera shutter, then sleekly glides into the next pose, cuter than the last.

Oh cat; I'd say, or pray: be-ooootiful cat!
Delicious cat! Exquisite cat! Satiny cat!
Cat like a soft owl, cat with paws like moths;
jeweled cat, miraculous cat!
Cat, cat, cat, cat.

Doris Lessing

God made the cat in order that man might have the pleasure of caressing the lion. Fernand Mery

Punkin does what he wants, when he wants, and how he wants, exuding much cattitude in the process.

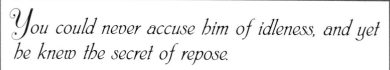

You could never accuse him of idleness, and yet he knew the secret of repose.

Charles Dudley Warner

Shakir is one crazy cat, who, if human, could be a contortionist. Is there such a thing as a *catortionist*?

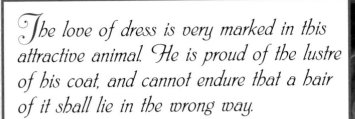

The love of dress is very marked in this attractive animal. He is proud of the lustre of his coat, and cannot endure that a hair of it shall lie in the wrong way.

Jules Chamfleury

Micio is constantly grooming. Lick, preen, lick again, and repeat as necessary until every hair is perfectly aligned and glistens with a rich sheen

> *Nothing can exceed the affection of a cat to those who treat it kindly.*
>
> — William Rhind

Louisa May Allcat would like some cream please. And make it snappy, she does not have all day. There are places to go and things to do. And while you are at it, she would also like you to brush her, rub her belly, and scratch behind her ears

> *A cat is there when you call her – if she doesn't have anything better to do.* Bill Adler

Parker likes to perch on the arbor, in close proximity to the bird feeder.
But the birds are wise to him now and fly off as soon as he appears.

> *If we treated everyone we meet with the same affection we bestow upon our favorite cat, they, too, would purr.*
>
> Martin Buxbaum

"S-t-r-e-t-c-h out those paws now, overhead and wide, now kick, and roll, and 1-2-3-4." Moki regularly demonstrates his callisthenic routine to the amusement of all.

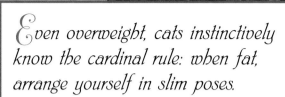

Even overweight, cats instinctively know the cardinal rule: when fat, arrange yourself in slim poses.

John Weitz

Tom had been on a diet for a year when this photo was taken. I was told not to laugh at him, as he is very sensitive. He moves daintily in his enormousness, always landing with white mittens touching, as if ready to perform an Olympic dive.

13

Kittens are born with their eyes shut. They open them in about six days, take a look around, then close them again for the better part of their natural lives.   Stephen Baker

One minute Minky, Blinky, and Muffin Puff were rolling and tussling. The very next minute the fur balls were fast asleep in kitten slumberland.

When you come upon your cat, deep in meditation, staring thoughtfully at something that you can't see, just remember that your cat is, in fact, running the universe.

Bonnie Elizabeth Hall (and Missy cat)

Lola showed up one day and plunked herself down as if to say, "I have always been here, it is you who just arrived."

Before a Cat will condescend
To treat you as a trusted friend,
Some little token of esteem
Is needed, like a dish of cream.

T.S. Eliot

Lap, lap, lap. Maki laps up her milk and licks her chops.
She then surveys her surroundings and glares at any other cat
expressing interest towards her large bowl of milk.

I believe cats to be spirits come to earth. A cat, I am sure, could walk on a cloud without coming through.

Jules Verne

Delicate Mitzi likes her water sparkling fresh and bubbly from the fountain. She turns her nose up at plain old still water in a bowl.

> *Meow is like aloha – it can mean anything.*
>
> Hank Ketchum

Meowko was born in Japan and moved to America.
She is a bilingual kitty-cat who can say "meow" in both English and Japanese.

> *The cat is nature's beauty.*
>
> French proverb

Michael slinks through the lily garden in a constant quest for amusement
and distraction. The slightest movement or noise sends him
pouncing in that direction.

*O*ne of the oldest human needs is having someone to wonder where you are when you don't come home at night.

Margaret Mead

Betty has the perfectly coiffed handlebar moustache of a distinguished gentleman... or someone who just slurped up their milk. From her perch below the pansy pot, she watches the world go by.

> *Anywhere!*
> *They don't care!*
> *Cats sleep*
> *Anywhere.*
>
> Eleanor Farjeon

We thought that Olivia was very intelligent, until we tried to teach her to use a magnetic cat door. My husband put food on the other side of the cat door, got on all fours, and demonstrated the head-bumping technique many times in the weeks it took to train her. Not so smart I thought, or was she? Perhaps Olivia was stalling for her own amusement.

> *Prowling his own quiet backyard or asleep by the fire, he is still only a whisker away from the wild.*
>
> Jean Burden

Watching us eat dinner is a favorite pastime of Skitty's.
He presses his nose so close to the window that it fogs up.
Then he paws off a circle of condensation so he can see us again.

If I called her she would pretend not to hear, but would come a few moments later when it could appear that she had thought of doing so first. Arthur Weigall

Mr. Tibbs is now on his tenth life in cat heaven. Even before he passed away, he often appeared to be communicating with the invisible realm.

> *What intenseness of desire*
> *In her upward eye of fire.*
>
> William Wordsworth

Flopsy seeks a few moments of peace, away from her housemate,
the ever-bothersome Izzy.

Kati is a petite package of fur. Despite her diminutive size, she has a fearsome meow that makes hair stand up on other cat's backs.

The cat sees through shut lids.

English saying

25

> *The smallest feline is a masterpiece.*
>
> Leonardo da Vinci

Cleo is a manx with a bit of a tail. She furiously waves that nubby stub,
as if to compensate for it not being full length.

> # *Cats are angels with fur.*
>
> Sark

Spoiled with the finest of everything, Pearl lives a delightful life of luxury.
She disdains the morning dew on her silky paws and navigates
the garden in a pattern of dewdrop avoidance.

Most cats, when they are Out
Want to be In,
And vice versa,
And often simultaneously.

Dr. Louis J. Camuti

Fred is as old
as the hills and
twice as wise.
He's been
around the
block more
than a few
times and
decided that
there is no
place like
home.

All animals are equal, but some animals are more equal than others.

George Orwell

Felix won me over quickly with his big personality. Before he lies down, he communicates via a nose to nose with his feline friends nearby.

One reason we admire cats is for their proficiency in one-upmanship. They always seem to come out on top; no matter what they are doing, Or pretend to do.

Barbara Webster

Sisters Tara and Clara look like twins as they strut on the wooden fence. When they try to pass one another on the narrow plank, one inevitably falls off. Composure is momentarily lost, but quickly she acts as if it never happened.

> *Cats are mysterious kind of folk. There is more passing in their minds than we are aware of.*
>
> Sir Walter Scott

Never-never land is where Tinkerbell often seems to be—a world of her own imagination and enjoyment.

The cat accepts your hospitality, but not your obligations. English saying

Katy often stands on her hind legs, like a prairie dog, to get a better look at the goings on next door. A new love interest on the other side of the fence? She'll never tell.

Sparkle and Gabby meet on the fence for a little cat-chat. They mew and meow, exchanging neighborhood gossip. Then they settle down for an afternoon nap.

A cat can purr its way out of anything.

Donna McCrohan

After scolding one's cat, one looks into its face and is seized by the ugly suspicion that it understood every word. And has filed it for reference.

Charlotte Gray

Calicat thinks she cannot be seen, hiding behind the hydrangea pot with both ends inconveniently protruding out.

Cats are kindly masters, just so long as you remember your place.

Paul Gray

Archy is not finicky, as long as he gets his water in the ivory ceramic bowl, and his food on the green china dish, from which he will remove it to devour it on the ground.

Cats can work out mathematically the exact place to sit that will cause most inconvenience.

Pam Brown

Kit-Cat holds court with a wizened expression and paws crossed regally one over another. Do not even think about sitting on his cushioned throne, or King Kit-Cat will be very displeased!

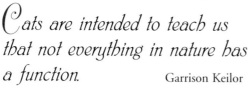

Cats are intended to teach us that not everything in nature has a function.

Garrison Keilor

I am perplexed by the physics relating to this, but I know that when a cat does not want to move it can seemingly double its weight. Tuffy is a master of instant density and mass gain.

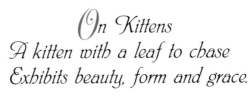

On Kittens
A kitten with a leaf to chase
Exhibits beauty, form and grace.

Salvatore Marsiglia

Snowshoe has an adventurous spirit. He climbs out on tree limbs, then can't get down. But that does not stop him from doing it again.

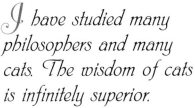

I have studied many philosophers and many cats. The wisdom of cats is infinitely superior.

Hippolyte Taine

Toes is an art cat. She lives with a painter who claims she helps him make aesthetic decisions by sitting next to the paint tube she thinks he should use, or staring at an area of the painting that needs more work.

> *She will attempt nothing that she cannot do well.*
>
> K.C. McIntosh

A study in tranquility, Cheva quietly sits and watches with large luminous eyes, for hours on end.

Smidgen rolls over and back in a display of momentary catnip abandon. "Ah, how nice it is to feel the warm sun on my back, and grass on my belly... or is that sun on my belly and grass on my back?"

The cat has nine lives — three for playing, three for straying, and three for staying.

English proverb

Her function is to sit and be admired.

Georgia Strickland Gates

I had a chance meeting with this prim, proper, and vain cat
who lived up to her name: Lady

> *If there is one spot of sun spilling onto the floor, a cat will find it and soak it up.*
>
> Joan Asper McIntosh

Behind the old wagon wheel is Boo-Boo's chosen spot. There he can sunbathe in peace, out of reach of all those pesky people who want to pet him.

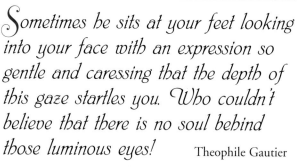

Sometimes he sits at your feet looking into your face with an expression so gentle and caressing that the depth of this gaze startles you. Who couldn't believe that there is no soul behind those luminous eyes!

Theophile Gautier

At home in a French garden bistro, Shiloh sports a clean white bib. He is ready to sample your leftovers, but would prefer if you ordered the filet of sole.

44

Cat said: "I am not a friend, and I am not a servant. I am the cat who walks by himself, and I wish to come into your cave." Rudyard Kipling

Stryder is an alert watch cat who stands at attention next to the iron dog statuettes.

She was occupied in her cat world, of all existences most secret and, no doubt, delightful.

Ethel Wilson

Brigitte lives in a Japanese garden with a Koi pond. From her rocky perch, she monitors the movement of the huge orange fish sliding through the water, hoping they will get too close.

46

You can always tell when Blanca is taking her morning, mid-morning, afternoon, mid-afternoon, and late afternoon nap because she snores with abandon.

Cats are rather delicate creatures and they are subject to a good many ailments, but I never heard of one who suffered from insomnia.

Joseph Wood Krutch

A cat can maintain a position of curled up somnolence on your knee until you are nearly upright. To the last minute she hopes your conscious will get the better of you and you will settle down again.

Pam Brown

Louie is looking for a lap. Any lap will do, even a stranger's.
Louie loves laps. Too bad people only have laps when they are sitting.

*Our perfect companions
never have fewer than four feet.*

Colette

Annabelle tags along at my feet and between my legs and on my toes.
I finally understand that she wants me to stand still, before she trips me,
so I can attend to her urgent need for stroking.

49

Louder he purrs and louder,
In one glad hymn of praise
For all the night's adventures,
For quiet restful days.

Alexander Gray

Mimosa has the loudest purr I have ever heard. He sounds like a well-tuned
machine humming away at full speed in his lovely dahlia courtyard.

50

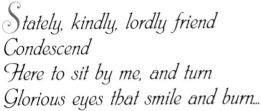

Stately, kindly, lordly friend
Condescend
Here to sit by me, and turn
Glorious eyes that smile and burn...

Algernon Charles Swinburne

Her round golden hypnotic eyes stare unblinkingly at the camera. Chili has a mellow disposition and patiently stands in place until I am done photographing her.

There are hundreds of good reasons for having a cat, but all you need is one.

A cactus greenhouse is Greystoke's home.
He has learned not to rub up against the cactus,
or the cactus rubs back — ouch!

A cat has absolute honesty.

Ernest Hemingway

Highly energetic George is an Abyssinian cat. Although he appears
in a moment of repose, he usually can be found in a paw batting match
with his nemesis and best friend, Blixen.

Of all animals, he alone attains to the *Contemplative Life.*

Andrew Lang

Josie is a very contented pussycat. She lounges about in a state of perfect serenity. We can all learn something from her satisfaction with life as it is.

Who could believe such pleasure from a wee ball o´ fur?

Irish saying

Bitsy is discovering everything all at once, including her whiskers.

It is a difficult matter to gain the affection of a cat. He is a philosophical, methodical animal, tenacious of his own habits, fond of order and neatness, and disinclined to extravagant sentiment. He will be your friend, if he finds you worthy of friendship. Theophile Gautier

Sultan strolls the grounds of an eighteenth century Italian farmhouse. In the mornings he can be found sitting on the windowsill awaiting his breakfast of fresh cream before he begins his daily rounds of rubbing up against legs.

*A little lion, small and dainty sweet...
With sea-grey eyes and softly stepping feet.*

Graham R. Tomson

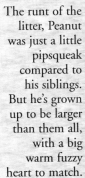

The runt of the litter, Peanut was just a little pipsqueak compared to his siblings. But he's grown up to be larger than them all, with a big warm fuzzy heart to match.

The Stray Cat

It's just an old alley cat that has
followed us all the way home.

. . .

"Beauty," we shall call you.
"Beauty, come in."

Eve Merriam

Wanda had a rough life before finding a place to call home. Still not sure if it is real, she keeps a wary eye out for danger, and startles easily at the slightest sound.

The ideal of calm exists in a sitting cat.

Jules Reynard

Miami is the essence of mellow. Set him down and he stays put as if to imply
that it is entirely too much effort to move on his own, even a paw.

Can the cat resist temptation any more than I can resist breathing?

Oscar Wilde

Squirrelly has the carefree attitude of a reckless teenager.
She darts about and flings herself into the air after
any winged creature, or nothing at all.

Cats have always been associated with the Moon. Like the Moon, they come to life at night, escaping from humanity and wandering over housetops with their eyes beaming out through the darkness. Patricia Dale Green

Every month during the full moon, Luna goes crazy — spinning around in circles like a lunatic. The rest of the time Luna usually lounges like this, with nary a care in the world.

You have now learned to see
That cats are much like you and me
And other people whom we find
Possessed of various types of mind.

T.S. Eliot

Sapphire lives on a houseboat at the end of a long dock.
She is a willynilly busy body who pokes her nose into everyone's business,
but does not want you to know hers.

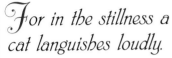

*For in the stillness a
cat languishes loudly.*

William Ernest Henley

Smoky lives
in a plant
nursery. She
knows all the
best places for
sun-basking.
Throughout
the day she
creeps along
slowly to
follow the
warm shafts of
golden light.

63

> *I had been told that the training procedure with cats was difficult. It's not. Mine had me trained in two days.*
>
> Bill Dana

Dizzy has a wayward whisker or two. In some cultures an aberrant whisker means good luck. In others, having a cat brings good luck. Dizzy embodies both of these beliefs simultaneously.

All cats are possessed of a proud spirit...

Michael Joseph

Lancelot is the neighborhood stud, always on the lookout for a female
to impress with his stunning fur coat and purr-fectionate ways.

Cat

Old Mag comes in and sits
on the newspaper
Old fat sociable cat
Thinks when we stroke him
he's doing us a favour
Maybe he's right, at that.

Joan Aiken

Whiskers makes quite a commotion if someone else wants to sit on his favorite old chair. The only way to appease him is to offer him a nice crisp newspaper to sit on.

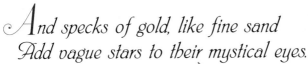

And specks of gold, like fine sand
Add vague stars to their mystical eyes.

Charles Baudelaire

Miki is a timid and cautious scaredy-cat, who keeps her distance. Ear radars constantly tuning, inform her when someone has unknowingly invaded her personal space.

> *A cat's eyes are windows enabling us to see into another world.*
>
> Irish Legend

Sparkle fixes her gaze beyond the object she is looking at,
as if looking right through it. Does she have a special ability to see
into another realm that only cats can perceive?

Cats seem a bridge to a world beyond the one we know.

Lynn Hollyn

Ebony is a young old soul who seems to contemplate on nothing
for hours on end. Under his panther-like blackish fur coat,
is a hint of stripes that just barely show through.

Is not a cat's middle name adventure?

Rudyard Kipling

Max races in a large circle around the garden perimeter, stopping every so often to look back at some invisible entity chasing him.

> *The tail in cats is the principal organ of emotional expression.*
>
> Aldous Huxley

Moving in slow motion, Gabby stalks prey imperceptible to the human eye. However, her excitement is betrayed by her madly quivering tail.

> *No matter how much cats fight, there always seem to be plenty of kittens.*
>
> Abraham Lincoln

Five little kittens knead their tiny mittens into Sheba's belly to get more milk. Afterwards, she'll resume licking and cleaning her squirming newborn fur balls.

The trouble with a kitten is
THAT
Eventually it becomes a
CAT

Ogden Nash

Miss Kitty plays king-of-the-tree with her siblings, Foxy, Moxy, and Puddin Pie, each morning before the day heats up. She's ready to rule for a moment or two, before being dethroned by a rival.

73

> *We humans are indeed fortunate if we happen to be chosen to be owned by a cat.*
>
> Anonymous

Aby, a rescue cat, lives in a sunny overgrown garden
full of flowers and fluttering distractions.
"What a good place to live at least one of my lives," thinks he.

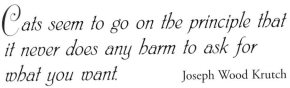

Cats seem to go on the principle that it never does any harm to ask for what you want.   Joseph Wood Krutch

Tux is a crooner who meows melancholy melodies, *M-ow-o-ah, mmm-ow, mmm-ow, ow-ow-ah.* This loosely translates as "Pet me, feed me, feed me, scratch me good."

75

In a cat's eyes, all things belong to cats.

English saying

Like an Egyptian sphinx, Beatrice lounges in front
of her house lazily guarding the portal.

> *Cats simply ought not to go about radiating such distracting charm.*
>
> Beverly Nichols

Winston is the undisputed alpha male cat. But then again, maybe he's not really so tough, as I watched him take time to smell a daisy.

Our Cat

The cat goes out
And the cat comes back
And no one can follow
Upon her track.
She knows where she's going,
She knows where she's been,
And all we can do
Is to let her in.

Marchette Chute

Chula seems to know
where she is going,
even if her meandering
appears to be random.

When the tea is brought at five o-clock
And all the neat curtains are drawn with care,
The little black cat with bright green eyes
Is suddenly purring there.

Pishker is an expert flycatcher. His head rolls around in a circular motion following the fly's flight path. Then *BOING* - straight up in the air he jumps and catches the hapless fly in his mouth.

True

When
the green eyes
of a cat
look deep into
you

you know
that
whatever it is
they are saying
is
true.   Lilian Moore

Kali is named
after a fierce,
earthy, and
compassionate
Indian goddess.

If man could be crossed with the cat it would improve man, but deteriorate the cat. Mark Twain

Sid eagerly awaits a tidbit of fresh salmon. It tastes best when it is served on the chipped blue plate from the top wooden step of the back porch.

His friendship is
not easily won
but it is something
worth having.

Michael Joseph

When I kneel
to tend garden,
Boots jumps
on my back
with paws
splayed out
front like rid-
ing a bicycle —
so I take him
for a scenic
kitty-back ride.

> *There are no ordinary cats.*
>
> Colette

Must keep those little paws white, white, white!
Buttons has meticulous grooming standards.
Over and over again he licks his fur until it shines.

> *...this mysterious, mystical, bundle of fur that won't come when you call it.*
>
> John Reynolds

Jade keeps cool under the peach tree. Every once in a while she comes out from underneath, looks around with her jade green eyes, and returns to her shady seclusion, satisfied that there is nothing worth staying awake for.

84

Thousands of years ago, cats were worshiped as gods. Cats have never forgotten this.

Smudge has the regal air of high rank or noble lineage. Cat-God? Furry deity?
He is indignant that we do not acknowledge his exalted status.

> *I love cats because I enjoy my home; and little by little, they become its visible soul.*
>
> Jean Cocteau

If he saw us looking his way, Rabbit would roll on his back and begin kneading the air with his paws to emphasize his cuteness, in hopes that we could not resist rubbing his belly—and we would, thus reinforcing the ritual.

All your wondrous wealth of hair,
Dark and fair,
Silken-shaggy, soft and bright
As the clouds and beams of night,
Pays my reverent hand's caress
Back with friendlier gentleness.

Algernon Charles Swinburne

Corsica is an aloof beauty. She flirts and preens and shows off
for attention, but scampers off when approached.

Only the spring breeze steps as lightly as a cat.

Theophile Gautier

Xena is a timid kitty with a warrior heart. Every day she explores her newfound territory a bit further, claiming it as her own.

Cats are better than any vice. They're not fattening, dangerous, or expensive. However, they can be addictive.

Snoop is a calico cat. Calico cats have tri-colored mottled markings, usually black, white, and orange. The name comes from printed cotton fabrics from Calicut, India, that traded as early as the sixteenth century.

Everything that moves serves to interest and amuse a cat.

F.A. Paradis De Moncrof

Perpetual motion Scamp. Even when seemingly still, some part of his body is twitching uncontrollably.

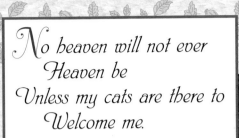

*No heaven will not ever
Heaven be
Unless my cats are there to
Welcome me.*

Epitaph in a pet cemetery

Puss' fate was
part of a sales
transaction.
The new
business owner
agreed to love
and care for
him to seal
the deal.

91

A rose has thorns, a cat has claws; certainly both are worth the risk.

Michael and Jason bask beside the pagoda in a lush garden of lilies and roses.
They raise their noses to sniff the aromas emanating from the blossoms.

92

*K*ittens believe that all nature
is occupied with their diversion.

F.A. Paradis De MonCrif

Peek-a-boo - I see you, is Cinnamon's favorite game.
She pops her head up from the flowerpot, and down again, all day.

If...
If you,
Like me.
Were made of fur
And sun warmed you,
Like me.
You'd purr.

Karla Kuskin

Marmalade likes to play, and play, and play — and eat, and eat, and eat.

> *Cats know everything there is to know about meditation.*
>
> Veronique Vienne

Buster meditates each morning, reflecting upon the warmth of a patch of sun, and the pleasure of a good scratch under the chin. He serenely holds his Buddha-like pose, until he hears the can-opener announce mealtime.